IS THIS BOOK REALLY FOR YOU?

This book is written for people who operate as small business owners of professional practices. These people are breadwinners for their families, serve as pillars of trust in our communities, and help form the backbone of our economies.

They also feel the impact of government taxation, get frustrated with their regulatory bodies, compete with big firms on a fraction of the marketing budget, and are preyed upon by people in marketing and advertising whose only interest is short-term gain.

The truth is, you're an expert in your professional field, not a business or marketing expert. No one taught you how to run a business or get great clients or patients – and it's not exactly a walk in the park.

It can be easier and it can be better. This book can help you make remarkable gains in your practice and design your life your way.

If your practice is running smoothly, performing well, and you have no real complaints – I'm glad to hear it. This book will give you ideas about how to take your practice from good to great.

If your practice isn't what you want it to be, your income is less than ideal, or you accept too many headache-inducing clients or patients, this book can help you change that. It can help you not just survive, but thrive.

You have the power to transform your practice into something more enjoyable, gratifying, and profitable.

I invite you to discover how.

Published 2019

Book design by Colin Noseworthy

www.ProvenMarketingForProfessionals.com

ISBN 978-1-9995712-0-7

THE
BIG PICTURE
GUIDE

TO BUILDING YOUR
DREAM PRACTICE

**Powerful
Lessons for
Professionals**

CATHERINE CROSBIE

WHAT PEOPLE SAY ABOUT CATHERINE CROSBIE

"We are a small personal injury law firm that recently faced the challenge of a name change and rebranding. Catherine Crosbie is our marketing consultant, and she managed our entire rebranding project. She planned and coordinated every aspect of the marketing assignment, including ensuring that all deadlines were met. She is extremely organized, efficient and detail-oriented. Most importantly, Catherine listened to our ideas, applied her expertise and knowledge in legal marketing, and delivered exactly what we envisioned. She is a true professional. We could not be happier with the result."

Darlene Russell, Russell Accident Law

"I have had the opportunity to work with Catherine on a number of occasions and I cannot speak more highly of her. She is a superior marketing strategist and will most definitely get the job done."

Bradley Russell, Political Consultant

"Catherine has provided excellent advice about yellow page advertising, location and branding. This advice has been a great help in making the transition from a partnership to a solo practice."

Geoff Aylward, AylwardLaw.ca

"Catherine has done a wonderful job helping my law firm successfully get off the ground with a practical, tailored marketing strategy. Highly recommended."

Mike Dull, Valent Legal

"Catherine was a great help with fine tuning my social media marketing strategies, proper pricing and wording to attract the right customers. With only advertising on two social media platforms, I was able to fully fill my yoga classes within two weeks and cover my equipment, contractor, marketing costs and pull a profit. I am very satisfied with the service & recommendations received. I would highly recommend Catherine as the marketing professional for your business ventures!"

Sabrina Belanger, True Strength Inc.

"I watched Catherine help grow Ches Crosbie Barristers through spectacular and highly effective marketing. She's been an excellent contributor to my organization's MasterMind group and is at the forefront of direct marketing for lawyers in Canada."

Ben Glass, Ben Glass Law

"I sold a personal injury practice along with marketing assets which included my name, but I was not ready to retire. The new owner did not wish to pursue the medical malpractice sub-specialty, but I did. Therefore I needed to re-position and rebrand consistent with the sale agreement and my marketing goals. Catherine took the rebranding strategy along with the detail stuff off my plate, so I could focus on the highest and best use of my time. She worked with my assistant to create an intake system, a new website with new content, social media, a targeted newsletter to my 6500 name list... you get the idea. Stuff that great lawyers should not have to do, because they are better off being great lawyers. Catherine is your reinvention one stop shop!"

Ches Crosbie, Patient Injury Law

"Catherine is a friendly, smart and hard-working marketing consultant who focuses on helping professionals grow their enterprises. Strategic marketing has been the core activity of my 46 years in the business world as an owner, consultant, senior manager and now the facilitator/coach of TAB Halifax. It is absolutely critical to long-term business success. Catherine intimately understands marketing. Her track record shows beyond doubt that she is of great help to professionals who want to build and maintain their clientele."

Geoff Tooton, Business Strategist

"Catherine Crosbie is one of the sharpest young minds in the lawyer marketing world. She is capable of both delivering new clients to a law practice by improving their marketing while also showing them how to build a long-term brand in their community. If I were a practicing lawyer in Canada, I would absolutely hire Catherine to work on or run my marketing."

Charley Mann, Great Legal Marketing

"Catherine is a gift to all Canadian lawyers who believe they're more than just lawyers, but are entrepreneurs and business people who can make a difference in people's lives... I've worked with Catherine for several years... She is not only knowledgeable in crafting a compelling message and communicating it to the market, but she's done it successfully over and over again. Catherine teaches proven marketing because she's done it and knows what works and what doesn't. Consider yourself lucky to work with her."

Kia Arian, Zine

"I have had the pleasure of working with Catherine on communication and marketing related tasks for a client. She is always professional, effective, responsive and organized. Any individual or firm would be lucky to have Catherine on their team."

Devin Drover, Political Consultant

"We had the privilege of working with Catherine this past year when she completed a Marketing Asset Assessment for our law firm. Catherine is extremely knowledgeable and provides ideas and strategies that are easy to implement. She is always pleasant and is very responsive. We recommend Catherine to any law firm looking for assistance in enhancing their marketing initiatives."

Shannon Leeper, Rastin & Associates

"Catherine is an excellent marketer and a lovely person to work with. She treats others with respect and has a great work ethic. I've seen her marketing skills firsthand and can say that she's a great choice for any Canadian lawyers looking for proven marketing strategies."

Bethany Jones, The Young Firm

"Looks like good coverage so far. I want to thank you so much for your outstanding work putting all the pieces of this media event together. Very professional, extremely well organized. Also your hard work and effort in helping to get people to attend. You are wonderful. Thank you so much."

Tom Murphy, Political Campaign Manager

"Catherine is professional, thoughtful, detail oriented and task driven. Catherine has a keen eye for marketing strategy and her dedication will show proven results! Highly recommended!"

Miriah Carpey, My HOME Apparel

"As someone who is responsible for writing a law firm newsletter, I always turn to Catherine's publications for great ideas. Her newsletters are not only relevant and informative, they are also heartfelt and genuine. I love the way they incorporate their lives outside of the office; it really gives the reader a sense of who they are dealing with. Catherine is an amazing author, produces awesome newsletters and press releases, and is an all-around great person who is highly organized and insightful. She will do wonders for any firm and I am proud to say I have used her guidance."

Anneke Godlewski, Charles E. Boyk Law Offices

"As the managing member of a small but national New York based law firm, I have had the opportunity to work with numerous professionals, advisors and consultants regarding law firm business development and marketing. Over the past number of years I have had the opportunity to directly work with Catherine Crosbie, participate in private conferences and events where our firm gained insights into the direct response client development strategies, programs and organic efforts that Catherine developed and utilized in building Ches Crosbie Barristers and, in many instances, adapt these strategies for our own law firm. For those interested in building a successful law firm practice that they are proud of - one that is honest and genuine in the commitment and promises that they make to their valued clients and one that is focused on building enduring long-term client relations - Catherine Crosbie and the consulting services that she offers represent the very best in the legal industry and a rare opportunity if you get to work with her."

Charles Internicola, The Internicola Law Firm, PC

"Catherine has assisted me in my businesses multiple times, which has led to positive outcomes each time that she has helped me. I can confidently say that: Catherine is extremely capable, intelligent, hard-working, and professional. She takes great care in her work, and is constantly striving to give her clients the best possible results to meet their needs."

John Good, Real Estate Investor

"I met Catherine several years ago in a mastermind group. She always had great insights and made valuable contributions to the group - which was made up of lawyers who were operating at an extremely high level in terms of marketing. When she went on her own I retained her to do some work for. She definitely knows what she's talking about and you can't go wrong getting her on your team."

Walter Reaves, Law Offices of Walter M. Reaves Jr.

"Catherine is extremely professional, respectful, and attentive with her work, and I would highly recommend working with her for all your marketing needs."

Jenny Jeffrey, Onside Performance Centre

"I have had the privilege to work with Catherine for the last two years and in an environment that was unlike any work that she been engaged in previously. To my delight, although not surprisingly, she not only adapted quickly to this new experi-ence but excelled at both creating and marketing our message, often in a creative and unique way. Our whole team began to

look to Catherine as the "go to" expert for our messaging and marketing strategy. Catherine is a keen observer, listener and collaborator with the ability to use these and other valuable tools to push and extend boundaries. I have been 100% satisfied with both her professional engagement as well as her results and for that reason, I highly recommend Catherine as an essential asset for your business development."

Robert Lundrigan, Political Campaign Manager

Catherine provides thoughtful, practical advice on marketing. She clearly has the expertize and applies it well to your individual marketing needs. I recommend taking advantage of the initial assessment she offers. You will benefit. I did. She has also been very helpful in conducting Webinars for OTLA which I greatly appreciated. Thank you Catherine!

Siona Sullivan, Sullivan Injury Law

I've known Catherine for years and recently had the opportunity to work with her on a couple of projects. She is a pleasure to work with, is timely, innovative and a reliable service provider. I highly recommend her.

Frank Tooton, Chartered Financial Consultant

I dedicate this book to my loving parents, Lois Hoegg and Ches Crosbie.

*Mom, thank-you for being my ethics advisor and
equipping me with a strong moral compass.*

*Dad, I am fortunate to have you as a mentor
in business and creative-thinking.*

I am always learning from you both.

TABLE OF CONTENTS

SPECIAL OFFER: Turn to page 67 for a valuable gift

HERE'S THE STORY

> "Edit your life frequently and ruthlessly. It's your masterpiece after all." **– NATHAN W. MORRIS**

I come from a family of lawyers, but I'm not a lawyer. Many moons ago, I took advice from one of my university professors and simply followed my interests. It led me to do a master's degree in politics and communication at the London School of Economics. Upon completion of the program, I returned to my hometown of St. John's, Newfoundland and Labrador ready to discover the working world of marketing and communications.

In fact, I was working at an agency when my father approached me with a job offer. He owned a boutique personal injury law firm called Ches Crosbie Barristers and was trying to "do it all" – his legal work, managing the business, and marketing the firm. He knew that marketing wasn't the best use of his time. Furthermore, it often ended up getting pushed to the wayside because he didn't have time to do it consistently. Wanting to avoid a shrinking market share, my father offered me the position of Marketing Director at Ches Crosbie Barristers.

I had reservations about working for my father – I wanted to make my own name. All things considered, it seemed like the right move at the time.

So here we had a boss hiring his daughter for a position that had never existed before. I knew exactly what it looked like, and boy, did I have something to prove. Not only did I prove it, I knocked it out of the park.

I was Marketing Director at Ches Crosbie Barristers for three years. During that time, we increased our target intake by 94%. My marketing management allowed Dad to focus on practicing law because he knew there was a reliable stream of cash flow cases coming in monthly. He even took more personal leisure, family, and travel time. In fact, in 2016 he achieved his goal of selling the practice.

The sale of Ches Crosbie Barristers presented me with the opportunity to help lawyer clients across North America with their marketing operations, which is exactly what I did. Positive reviews poured in and soon I received inquiries and requests from other professionals who wanted to grow their practices.

Three years after I started Proven Marketing for Lawyers Inc I decided to expand and rename my business Proven Marketing for Professionals. Now I work with professional practices mostly in law, financial services, and health services.

Basically, I help professionals with marketing and business development so they can build their dream practices without the risk, expense, and hassle of hiring an in-house marketing director. I'm Canada's only education-based marketing consultant exclusively for professionals. I work from my new hometown of Halifax, Nova Scotia.

That's my story, but the rest of this book is not about me. It's about professionals like you, and the big picture of building your dream practice. Read on to discover why you deserve the lifestyle you've always wanted and how to turn it into a reality.

YOU WERE MADE TO THRIVE

> "Even at the lowest-level jobs, your success waits within your own mind. Add value to your work and you set in motion the forces that make the concepts of your mind turn into the realities of living." **– NAPOLEON HILL**

I get interesting reactions from people when I tell them about my business. I would even characterize some of these reactions as outrageous.

One time, a friend took me to a networking event for local tech start-ups. I thought it would be fun to tag along. At some point I was chatting with a woman who was starting a tech company, and when she asked me what I did for a living I told her marketing for lawyers. This was before I expanded to work with other professionals.

"Pfff," she scoffed. "Do lawyers even need more money?"

I was shocked. First of all, yeah, some lawyers do need more money. As many readers know, being a lawyer or any other professional for that matter is far from having a license to print cash.

More importantly, what I do is not just about making money. It's about helping people obtain their own definitions of success. These usually involve autonomy, prosperity, free time, and gratification.

Despite what some think, I believe that supporting others in achieving their goals is a worthy cause. I love helping people design their lives their way and I feel privileged to accompany them on their journeys.

This is not the only time that someone has reacted rudely to what I do. It will not be the last, either.

People like this have a certain way of thinking – a scarcity mentality. They believe life is like a pie and when someone takes a slice there is less pie for everyone else. In other words, they believe there is a finite amount of success in the world and we are all competing for it.

The other way of thinking is called an abundance mentality. People with an abundance mentality believe there are endless ingredients for pie-making; we need not ration because there is always a way to make more. In other words, success is available to anyone who wants to create it. Expressions like "a rising tide lifts all boats" and "win-win solutions" capture the sentiment.

People with an abundance mentality believe that everyone – lawyers, tech geeks, accountants, therapists, you name it – is made to thrive.

Take my father, for example. He wasn't made to sit in a cubicle and do legal work that he hated. He was made to creatively solve client problems, make a meaningful difference in people's lives, shape Canadian law, serve the emotional and financial well-being of his family, and enjoy the journey.

Look at Michelle Moller, owner of Basin View Family Dentistry (and yes, that is her real name). She wasn't made to clock in at 9 am, do standard dental work, and clock out at 5 pm. She was made to manage people, oversee systems, and provide high-level dental care. The result is happy, healthy patients and an efficient, scalable business.

Darlene Russell is the lawyer who bought Ches Crosbie Barristers, and with my planning and support, later rebranded it Russell Accident Law. She wasn't made to process files that other lawyers don't want and work 12-hour days. She was made to build relationships with good people who need legal help and run a successful firm that gives her the autonomy and prosperity she desires.

Consider Laurie Stephenson who owns Starboard Wealth Planners. She wasn't made to live by other people's rules. She was made to set higher standards, make her own rules, and help people grow their wealth through socially responsible investing.

Jim Dodson who owns Jim Dodson Law is another example. He wasn't made to miss family dinner six days a week and build a mediocre law firm. He was made to build a law business which enables him to raise a loving family, live an active lifestyle, and help like-minded people with their legal issues.

These people were made to thrive. We were all made to thrive!

I believe that entrepreneurship and business ownership offer professionals incredible opportunity. With the right mindset and systems, it enables professionals to control their own lives.

Furthermore, it enables a work life that serves their lifestyle, not the other way around. It gives them the chance to create their dream practices and a means to truly "have it all" – autonomy, prosperity, time, and gratification. This is attainable for almost anyone regardless of gender, background, age, or orientation. Proven Marketing for Professionals exists to support this cause and help professionals bring their dreams to life.

That's why my mission is to be the best marketing resource for owners of small professional practices in Canada, and that's why I've written this guide.

This guide is the best starting point for professionals who wish to design their lives their way. It's also a great reset tool for people who get distracted on their journeys to success.

If you're ready to design your life your way or get back on the path to achieving your goals, this guide contains foundational success principles to put you in the right mindset. It also gives practical how-to tips to get you started.

This guide does not try to sell my proven marketing services, nor does it contain information about them. However, it does give you an understanding of how I think so that if you find yourself interested in marketing support along the way, you'll know whether we're a good fit.

SUCCESS PRINCIPLE #1:
IGNORE THE NAYSAYERS

> "New opinions are always suspected, and usually opposed, without any other reason but because they are not already common." **– JOHN LOCKE**

There are people who will doubt you, pollute your thinking, speak ill of you, create obstacles, and even try to stop you, consciously or unconsciously, from building your dream practice. They are the naysayers. You cannot let them affect you.

The person from the networking event who I described in the previous chapter is a naysayer. This is the type of naysayer who is easy to identify and keep at a distance. Unfortunately, naysayers come in different forms, some of which are not so easy to identify or keep away.

Oftentimes, naysayers are among those closest to you, including family members and friends. They care about you, but cast doubt on what you can accomplish. They may be worried about your financial future and how it impacts *them*. They may be concerned about how your ambitions and actions will affect *their* social standing. They may be jealous. Sometimes they just don't understand.

Instead of seeing opportunities, they see road blocks. Instead of seeing potential, they see risk. Instead of seeing win-win solutions, there can only be one winner. Often, they're just more comfortable with tradition, convention, and maximum security.

You, the owner, are the only person who can and must be the visionary for your practice. You cannot reach your potential unless you learn to ignore the naysayers and move forward with confidence.

SUCCESS PRINCIPLE #2: KNOW YOUR PURPOSE

> "There is no real excellence in all this world which can be separated from right living." **– DAVID STARR JORDAN**

Your purpose is a statement about what gives your life meaning. It is highly personal and not intended for sharing, but you can share it if you want. This is not to be confused with a business purpose, which is a marketing asset intended for sharing.

Knowing your personal purpose brings clarity and motivation to daily life. It also helps you design a work life and set boundaries to serve your purpose.

One example of a purpose statement is "to provide financial and emotional support to my family". This comes from a law firm owner with many family members, some of whom have serious psychological issues. A long time ago, he decided to build a great law firm to serve his purpose. Today, he has more than enough financial resources to take care of his family and plenty of time to spend with them, too.

Another example of a purpose statement is "to make meaningful, enduring contributions to my community while living the best expression of myself." The woman who this belongs to is building her business around this purpose.

Knowing what gets you out of bed in the morning enables you to focus on what's most important. It provides perspective and helps you make the best decisions.

WHAT'S YOUR PURPOSE? USE THE SPACE
PROVIDED TO BRAINSTORM.

SUCCESS PRINCIPLE #3: PLAN STRATEGICALLY

> "One day Alice came to a fork in the road and saw a Cheshire cat in a tree. 'Which road do I take?' she asked. 'Where do you want to go?' was his response. 'I don't know,' Alice answered. 'Then,' said the cat, 'it doesn't matter." **– LEWIS CARROLL, ALICE IN WONDERLAND**

There's an expression that goes, "You get where you aim". If you aim high, you'll be a high achiever. If you aim low, you'll be a low achiever. If you're aimless, you'll achieve little or nothing. It's harsh – but true! That's why it's critical to know where you want to go and create a plan to get there. I call this process planning strategically.

Planning strategically involves creating a vision, mission, key performance indicators, and goals. This chapter briefly explains each component of planning strategically and challenges you to start the process. While this chapter is short, the process is not. It's normal to need a couple months to finalize this exercise.

I should note that my advice to plan strategically is inspired by the process of doing a strategic plan, but these are not the same. Doing a strategic plan goes much deeper than what I share here and there are people far more expert than I who facilitate strategic plans. I would also like to thank Laurie Sinclair from Nova Scotia's Centre for Women in Business for introducing me to much of this material.

We start with vision. The universal rule of planning is that you will never be greater than the vision that guides you. No Olympic athlete gets to the Olympics by mistake, and no professional accidentally stumbles upon their dream practice. You must decide what you want your life to look like five years from now. As author Stephen Covey writes, "Begin with the end in mind."

Once you have a vision, creating a mission grounds you in the practical day-to-day work so that you can see the path forward. It's a short statement of who you are and what you do. Your mission may be best expressed using the following template:

My mission is to provide/produce _____ to/for _____ by so that I can/in order to _____.

Next, you need key performance indicators (KPIs). KPIs are metrics that measure your performance in some capacity. Once you have a clear way of measuring it, you'll be able to make changes in your practice to enhance performance.

KPIs have four categories: finance, client value, internal systems, and growth and innovation. They can be quantitative or qualitative, as long as you can track and evaluate results. Here are examples of KPIs that may be relevant to you:

- Number of inquiries made per month
- Monthly revenue
- Monthly expenses
- Percent increase in revenue
- Percent decrease in expenses
- Percent increase in profit

- Percent increase in price
- Amount earned per hours worked
- Percent of client invoices paid
- Positive feedback from clients
- Number of referrals
- Number of repeat clients
- Number of online reviews
- How many existing clients purchased an upgraded service
- Number of staff people with stellar performance reviews
- E-newsletter open rate
- Website bounce rate
- Action items from professional development
- Networking opportunities taken
- Number of new strategic partnerships

As you can see, there are dozens of KPIs to choose from. I just listed the ones that came to mind first! Choose only those which are most useful at this stage. I recommend having one or two in each of the four categories and tracking them quarterly.

Your goals are last, but not least. Set your first few goals by creating targets for your KPIs. When you achieve your targets or change your KPIs, set new targets. You'll also want to set short and long-term goals for your overall career, health, personal life, family, finances, and relationships. Write them down so that you can reference them, revise them when appropriate, and stay focused. Here are a few examples of goals to set for your professional practice:

- Monthly, quarterly, and annual intake goals
- Launch a new practice area or service

- Hire a new superstar staff person so you can work less
- Get 20 Google reviews in the next three months
- Launch an annual initiative that benefits the community while increasing your local profile
- Build relationships with journalists to get featured in more media
- Improve management and performance so you can start taking more and longer vacations
- Sell the practice and retire by age 65

Remember, this chapter is short, but the strategic planning process is not. Instead of getting overwhelmed, write down what comes to mind first at the end of this chapter. Then revisit it periodically during the next few weeks until you have a vision, mission, KPIs, and goals. Your dream practice will come to life much sooner if you invest in strategic planning now.

People who make a priority of achieving their own definition of success tend to use resources and support systems along the way. Coaching is one such resource. If you're interested in exploring the benefits of having an executive coach, I know several professionals who have worked with Samy Chong. I have worked with him myself. Known as the "Corporate Philosopher", Samy became an executive coach to help other leaders solve their greatest challenges and find deeper meaning in life and work. Email him at samychong@rogers.com. He will be delighted to learn that I connected you.

Accountability groups are another great resource, of which Great Legal Marketing (GLM) is one. I encourage lawyers all over North America to discover success stories at **CatherineLovesGLM.com** and sign up for an introductory membership.

The Alternative Board (TAB) is another great option for all professionals and business owners looking to accelerate their success. Search "The Alternative Board" online to find a group near you.

WHAT DO YOU WANT YOUR LIFE TO LOOK LIKE IN FIVE YEARS?

WHAT'S YOUR MISSION? COMPLETE THE TEMPLATE AND USE THE SPACE BELOW TO BRAINSTORM.

My mission is to provide/produce _____

_____

_____

to/for _____

_____

_____

by _____

_____

_____

so that I can/in order to _____

_____

_____

WHICH KEY PERFORMANCE INDICATORS WOULD BE MOST USEFUL FOR YOU RIGHT NOW? LIST ONE OR TWO IN EACH CATEGORY.

Finance _____

_____

Client Value _____

_____

_____

Internal Systems _____

_____

_____

Growth and Innovation _____

_____

_____

WHAT ARE SOME OF YOUR SHORT AND
LONG-TERM GOALS PERTAINING TO
CAREER, HEALTH, PERSONAL LIFE, FAMILY,
FINANCES, AND RELATIONSHIPS?

SUCCESS PRINCIPLE #4: TAKE CARE OF YOURSELF FIRST

> "Private victories precede public victories. You can't invert that process any more than you can harvest a crop before you plant it." **– STEPHEN COVEY**

If you've been to law school, you're familiar with the lesson to put client interests before your own. Professional associations reinforce this mindset. I don't know how deeply ingrained this teaching is in other professional institutions, but one thing is clear – professionals across the board regularly sacrifice their own needs to serve clients and patients.

It's understandable because professionals have fiduciary duty. However, I respectfully insist that putting yourself anywhere but first contributes to dysfunctional business practices, unhealthy lifestyles, and unhappiness. Furthermore, it does little or nothing to benefit clients. In fact, putting yourself first while implementing systems to manage client expectations would do more to benefit clients.

If you've ever travelled with Air Canada, you've watched their in-flight safety video and heard the instruction, "Put on your own oxygen mask before assisting other passengers". Basically, they're saying that it's essential to take care of yourself first. Only when your needs are met are you in a position to help others. This rule applies not just to in-flight safety, but life in general!

Why, then, should professionals forfeit their own well-being and even jeopardize their own survival as a professional when they will inevitably run out of resources to help the people to whom they've made commitments?

I see my professional and business-owner friends sacrifice themselves all the time. They skip hard-to-get medical appointments to attend client meetings and routinely choose not to take income in order to make payroll. These are unsustainable practices which turn into lose-lose situations over time.

Without a profitable practice (or the makings of a profitable practice), and without your mental, physical, and emotional health, you will not have the resources to contribute to others' well-being. You will be "running on fumes", so to speak, and those fumes will eventually dissipate. That's why you owe it to your clients, employees, family, and yourself to put you first.

Jeff Bezos is the founder and CEO of Amazon, one of the most successful companies in the world, which has created large-scale disruptive change across multiple industries. It's easy to imagine the enormous pressures of running a company like Amazon and positioning it for continued success. Despite all these pressures, Bezos makes it a priority to get eight hours of sleep every night. He knows that adequate rest is essential to quality decision-making.

Think about my reference to abundance mentality a couple of chapters back. You have the power to create win-win solutions for your clients, employees, family, and yourself – all at the same time – without compromising adherence to professional and ethical standards. No one has to suffer. All you have to do is reflect on your current practices and implement changes to support winning solutions for yourself and those to whom you have commitments.

Controlling your calendar is a big part of taking care of yourself first. The last thing you want is your calendar controlling you. Block off time for what's most important in your life. Then book remaining time for working on the business, managing staff, client meetings or patient appointments, and so on.

No matter how busy I am, I block off time for the things that keep me grounded and in good form. These include getting enough sleep, regular exercise, and family dinner. While I may lose a good night's sleep or miss yoga practice every now and again, these general practices help me manage a healthy lifestyle and ensure that I'm able to give clients my best work.

Here are a few ideas to help you take care of yourself first:

- Stop working and turn off all electronics one hour before bed so that you fall asleep more easily.
- Block off enough time for eight hours of sleep every night.
- Exercise regularly and make healthy eating choices.
- See the doctor and dentist for routine check-ups and specialist appointments.
- Create a screening process so that you only accept business that is both profitable and enjoyable.

- Don't give out your cell phone number to clients. Instead, have an assistant evaluate whether matters in question are urgent. Most of the time, these issues can be addressed in a scheduled call or meeting.
- Use "out of office" email alerts when you're unavailable. Trying to answer every email while you're on vacation is not much of a vacation.
- Don't check your email during family or social time. Not only are you telling your family and friends that they're not a priority, checking email without giving it your full attention is an inefficient use of your time.
- Take time off to recoup emotional energy. This relates to weekends, vacations, holidays, and mental health days. Time off also gives you opportunity to think about the strategic direction of your practice and whether you're on track to meet your goals and bring your vision to life.
- Take advantage of support services through professional associations and other groups.
- As lawyer Siona Sullivan says, keep your sense of humour!

WHAT CAN YOU DO DIFFERENTLY TO START PUTTING YOURSELF FIRST?

SUCCESS PRINCIPLE #5: DEVELOP A MARKETING MENTALITY

| "The Secret is the 'mental' thing." **– BEN GLASS**

Most people have heard the saying, "build it and they will come." The problem is, it's BS.

Just because you start building a practice does *not* mean clients or patients will magically appear. It just doesn't work like that. You may know this by now.

Clients and patients appear because they know or heard about you, and they're convinced that you can solve their problems. They do not decide to hire you for the mere reason that you exist.

Dan Kennedy is a famous marketing advisor for small businesses and one of my favourite authors. His nicknames include "the millionaire-maker" and "Professor of Harsh Reality". He says that no matter what business you *think* you're in (lawyers tend to think they're in the business of law, accountants tend to think they're in the business of accounting, and so on), you're wrong. You're in the marketing business.

In other words, if you cannot leverage your relationships and use media to convince people to "buy" from you, you have no business at all.

I have to agree with Dan on this. Like it or not, you're in the marketing business!

If we accept that every business is in the marketing business, we must develop a marketing mentality. Marketing opportunities arise all the time – you just have to learn to see them. In fact, you can learn to see *everything* as a marketing opportunity.

Stuart Carpey is a Pennsylvania-based personal injury lawyer and the owner of Carpey Law. I distinctly remember something he said during a Great Legal Marketing mastermind meeting. It was, "You are *always* marketing". Taken within the context of his presentation, he meant that everything you do is an opportunity for, and reflection of, your practice.

Stuart's statement compliments another expression I read recently. Menna Riley is an event coordinator in Halifax, Nova Scotia and the founder of a women's networking group I belong to called Leading Ladies. Her website homepage mennariley. com says, "Ready to stake your reputation on your next event? Because you're already doing it." It couldn't be truer. The op- portunity is right in front of you. The time is now.

It goes without saying that you can't just think about marketing. You have to *do* it. That means you have to invest time, effort, and money in smart marketing.

Keep in mind I said *smart* marketing. I'll be the first to admit that lots of marketing is a waste of resources. Furthermore, there are "marketing vultures" out there who present scams and tricks as magic business-generating solutions. Buyer beware.

The best way to make sure you're investing in smart marketing is to measure your results. Remember that the best metric is return on investment (ROI).

I meet with prospects and clients all the time who don't have a formal tracking system. If they do, they often don't use the data on which they've spent valuable resources to collect. They file it away and forget that it can help them achieve their goals.

Shortly after starting my job as Marketing Director at Ches Crosbie Barristers, we came very close to getting rid of one particular advertising platform. The media organization was frustrating to work with and we were convinced it was a dying medium. Just before we were ready to pull out, we had a change of heart. We thought, hey, let's be smart about this. We'll set up our own call tracking account and give our ad a unique tracking phone number. At the end of the advertising cycle, we'll know for sure it's not working and be able to cancel with confidence. We couldn't have been more wrong!

After tracking our ad on this particular platform, we discovered it was well-worth the investment. When we implemented tracking for all of our media, we discovered the platform in question was one of our top intake sources. Pulling out would have been a huge mistake.

In summary, the key take-away points from this chapter are:

- Regardless of the services you provide, you're in the marketing business.
- Learn to see everything as a marketing opportunity.

- Don't just think about marketing, do it.
- Invest in smart marketing by tracking your results and using them to make better decisions.

THINK OF THE REGULAR ACTIVITIES IN YOUR
DAY-TO-DAY LIFE. WHAT ARE THE INHERENT
MARKETING OPPORTUNITIES? HOW CAN
YOU TAKE ADVANTAGE OF THEM?

SUCCESS PRINCIPLE #6: TARGET YOUR AVATAR

> "You can't create effective marketing without deciding whom you want to see walking through your office door as a result of that marketing." – **BEN GLASS**

There are different types of intake in every practice. You can label them in several ways, such as those you like or dislike; those which are profitable or take more effort than they're worth; and those which make your life easy or difficult.

Your "avatar" is your ideal client or patient. You may know him or her as the 20% of your practice that generates 80% of your revenue and 99% of your satisfaction, or something to that effect.

Someone with a scarcity mindset might say that any practice is bound to have a combination of good and not-so-good intake. Maybe it's because conventional business models insist you must earn the good by working with the bad. Maybe it's because there aren't enough avatars out there for everyone. Maybe it's because people in the community will start gossiping if you turn away too many people who are not a perfect fit.

Someone with an abundance mindset would say that you are the perfect professional for a certain type of client or patient, and that is the person who you exist as a professional to serve. Anyone else is a distraction from doing excellent work and making a meaningful difference in people's lives. The idea that newer professionals have to suffer to get to the top is nonsense. There are plenty of different people out there looking for the perfect professional service for them. Prospects who aren't the right fit will be grateful if you point them in the direction of someone who *is* right for them.

To build a practice of avatars, you must speak directly to them in your marketing. The moment you implement clear communications crafted specifically to the fraction of people you want to attract is the moment you'll start attracting more of them.

So, how do you implement clear communications crafted specifically to your avatar? It starts by getting to know your avatar *really* well. You should know their demographics including age, income, work, and family. You should know their interests and goals. And you should know what keeps them up at night. With this information, you can present solutions to their problems in the right tone and language to show that you're a perfect fit.

If you cannot articulate the person for whom you are the perfect professional and speak directly to them, they probably won't find you. Be clear about who you want to work with.

COMPETE THIS WORKSHEET TO GET TO KNOW YOUR AVATAR CLIENT OR PATIENT:

What is your avatar's gender?

How old is your avatar?

What is your avatar's education?

What does your avatar do for work?

What is your avatar's income range?

What is your avatar's relationship status?

What does your avatar's family look like?

What are your avatar's key personality traits? (Ex. Sense of humour, risk-taker, people-person…)

_____

What does the average day look like for your avatar?

_____

How does your avatar spend most of his or her time?

_____

How does your avatar spend his or her down time?

_____

What does your avatar like to do for fun?

_____

What interests your avatar?

_____

What are your avatar's core values?

_____

What does your avatar aspire to?

_____

What keeps your avatar awake at night?

_____

What does your avatar want from you?

_____

What does your avatar want from you without knowing it?

_____

How can you offer to calm your avatar's fears and give them what they want?

_____

What objections does your avatar have to hiring you?

_____

How can you overcome your avatar's objections?

_____

SUCCESS PRINCIPLE #7: SHOW UP LIKE NO ONE ELSE

> "In a crowded marketplace, fitting in is a failure. In a busy marketplace, not standing out is the same as being invisible." **– SETH GODIN**

Think of how other professional practices in your industry present. Whether you're in legal, financial, or health services, think about your competition. From a marketing perspective, do any of them stand out?

The reality is that most marketing for professional practices, even across jurisdictions, is remarkably similar. That is to say that most law firms look the same; most accounting firms look the same; most dental practices look the same.

For example, law firms everywhere seem to advertise on television or billboards for "all your legal needs" and brand themselves as tough or aggressive. Accounting firms often use some bland expression about dedication or experience. Dentists go on about complete oral health. Blah blah blah.

These firms may be attracting a sufficient number of prospects, but I'm willing to bet they're also wasting a ton of money and not getting the quality intake and profit margin they'd like.

To be fair, most professionals are not marketers or business people – they're experts in law, accounting, dentistry, and so on. Your training did not teach you how to market and build a successful business. Furthermore, regulatory bodies limit what you can say and do. No wonder everyone gravitates to the same old stuff.

I'm here to tell you that there's a better way.

This better way involves "showing up like no one else" because the truth is, you have to be different to stand out. You can do this using three different methods: market, message, and media. Ideally, you'll find ways to use all of three them. I'll share examples for each.

Before I do, I ask my non-lawyer readers to excuse me for using examples mainly about lawyers. While many of these examples relate to legal marketing, keep in mind that marketing principles are the same for all professional practices. The following examples are relevant to you, too.

My father's law firm, Patient Injury Law, is a great example of showing up like no one else to a particular market. Patient Injury Law is the *only* medical malpractice and class action-exclusive law firm in Newfoundland and Labrador. My father uses his unique skill and thought leadership in medical malpractice and class action law to seek justice for his clients, so they get the compensation and closure they deserve.

His practice is not just a niche, it's a sub-niche. Furthermore, as the only lawyer with this exclusive focus, he is in a "category of one". To compare him to anyone would be like comparing apples to oranges. People in Newfoundland and Labrador who think they have a medical malpractice or class action case, if they've done any research at all, will immediately discover that Ches Crosbie at Patient Injury Law is the go-to authority.

Hoffheimer Family Law, a firm based in Virginia Beach, offers another example of showing up like no one else to a market. Hoffheimer Family Law is for women only! This is not an experiment – they have been helping women only for a long time and choosing to do so was one of the most profitable decisions these lawyers ever made. Women seeking advice about family law in Virginia Beach and beyond discover very quickly there is one law firm that is expert at helping people just like them.

Hoffheimer Family Law is doing something else you might find interesting. They created an online service called Design your Divorce for women who don't feel they have enough money to hire an attorney. It's a quality service that provides attorney-written and jurisdiction-specific advice and forms. While it serves as a legitimate option, most of the women who sign up for this service end up realizing part-way through just how complicated divorce is. That's when many of them hire a lawyer from Hoffheimer Family Law. Not only does Design your Divorce give the firm a passive revenue stream, it delivers clients who wouldn't normally hire them (or anyone).

Applying the "show up like no one else" principle to your marketing message is also highly effective. Some might say it's essential. Dan Kennedy, for example, says that "Head-to-head competition is almost always bloody, costly and destructive to profitability. Better to re-define, so as to have no direct competition." That puts things in perspective.

Saying something different, especially to a targeted group of people, is a powerful strategy. When done well, it makes you memorable and persuades people to contact you. I recommend having various compelling messages which differentiate you and represent your authentic personality and approach. These messages include a unique selling proposition (USP), brand story, statement of business purpose, mission statement, core values, and guarantee. I'll share examples for context.

Domino's Pizza is known for having had a successful USP. It goes, "Fresh hot pizza delivered to your door in 30 minutes or less or it's free." This statement makes four promises. It promises that you will get 1) fresh pizza 2) hot pizza 3) you will get it within 30 minutes of ordering, and 4) if Domino's doesn't deliver all of the above, your pizza will be free. That's a pretty compelling offer, especially for university students. Not only did this statement differentiate Domino's from all of its pizza-delivery competitors, integrating a guarantee made it all the more persuasive.

You may be thinking, "I'm not allowed to use guarantees". Ultimately, you know your regulating body better than I do. If you think that using a guarantee is too risky, don't do it. However, it is possible to create a guarantee that meets ethical standards and passes muster with regulatory bodies. For example, Mike Dull at Valent Legal uses the following:

If you are not completely satisfied with the legal service at Valent Legal, or you are simply unhappy in the way we are handling your case, you can walk away any time within the first 90 days of our relationship – no questions asked. Our 100% guarantee means that you won't owe us anything at all. No fees. No costs. No kidding.

Here's another USP that I created for a client: "The *only* law firm in Newfoundland and Labrador that works exclusively to help car accident and personal injury clients. Our unique, in-depth experience helps us deliver the best possible outcome for clients and their loved ones." You can see how this statement differentiates the firm from all of their competitors.

Let's consider one more message. Walter Reaves is a criminal defence lawyer in Waco, Texas with a powerful mission statement. He says, "Our mission is to treat every client like a member of our family". This statement, followed by a sincere phone or in-person consultation, is a great way to stand out and attract clients.

Last but not least, the way you use media can also help you show up like no one else and capture people's attention. You can think of this as advertising where few others do.

You may well know, professionals weren't always allowed to advertise. In Newfoundland and Labrador, it was 1989 before lawyers could advertise their law practices. When the rules changed, my father was the first lawyer to advertise in the Yellow Pages. In fact, he was the only lawyer in the Yellow Pages for some time because advertising was still taboo after is was permitted. The reality is, he was showing up in a space with *no competitors*, which was of great benefit to him.

As I write this, the print Yellow Pages is once again of substantial benefit to professionals in certain markets (yes, you read that correctly). As people wrongly assume print is dead and transfer their resources into advertising on the overcrowded internet, I have to wonder why so few people see the new opportunity in a once again underutilized book.

Creating your own media such as newsletters, reports, magazines, books, podcasts, live casts, and more is a great way to show up like no one else. Each of these media have their own associated strategy. When used properly, they enable you to fill the minds of undistracted prospects with your personality and solutions. They keep you top of mind as prospects come to know, like, and trust you. By the time prospects are ready to hire, your products have made you the go-to resource.

HOW ARE YOU UNIQUE? HOW CAN YOU USE MARKET, MESSAGE, AND MEDIA TO SHOW UP LIKE NO ONE ELSE? USE THE SPACE BELOW TO BRAINSTORM.

SUCCESS PRINCIPLE #8: PRESENT YOURSELF AS AN AUTHORITY

> "Everybody perceived as big by their audience has a robust, expansive, comprehensive media 'ecosystem' of their own, typically integrating off-line and online: off-line including newsletters, magazines, books, information products, catalogs, annually or periodically updated resources, and much more; online including websites, members only sites, written word items, video items, PowerPoint slide presentations, introductory (free preview) courses, e-zines, e-books, email, catalogs/e-commerce stores, and more. If you do not have this, you aren't BIG."
>
> **– DAN KENNEDY**

There's always a handful of people who rise to the height of their fields. You know the leading authorities in your niches and professions. Many of these people aren't just celebrities within their professional communities – they have discovered how to leverage their reputability to show *prospects* that they are the go-to authority in their fields.

I've had the pleasure of getting to know a lawyer who is widely considered one of Canada's experts in his practice area. I'm naturally interested in how successful lawyers built their reputations and practices, so I asked him about how he became known as an expert. Hilariously, he said he just pretended to be an expert from the start.

The truth is, this man became an expert through a lot of study and hard work. He also sought out opportunities to *look* like an expert. These opportunities included speaking at conferences, making presentations, sitting on boards, and playing leading roles in professional associations. Even if he didn't know anything about the subject on which he was meant to speak, he figured it out in time.

Another lawyer I know, Reid Weingarten, has an equally interesting story. Reid is a world-famous white collar criminal defence lawyer and partner at Steptoe & Johnson LLP. When we last spoke, he had 30 lawyers working under him. The walls of his D.C. office are covered with framed newspaper articles about his notorious clients and their high-profile court proceedings. When I asked him how he became one of America's top criminal defence lawyers he said, "I got lucky".

The truth is, one of Reid's early cases got a lot of media attention which gave him momentum. However, he was able to leverage that media attention into much more. Everyone gets lucky once in a while. The game-changer is what we do with the opportunity.

The two stories above point out various tactics to help you become a leading authority. Below I list them and include others.

1.   Focus on a niche
2.   Speak at conferences
3.   Make presentations at professional and community events
4.   Sit on a board of directors
5.   Play a leading role in a professional association

6. Do interviews with the press
7. Author articles and white papers for your professional community
8. Market your practice or service areas separately
9. Author your own blog
10. Self-publish reports and books
11. Create webinars, podcasts, and live casts
12. Ask for reviews and testimonials

Note that you don't have to wait for other people to give you spotlight. In fact, you *shouldn't* wait on anyone to give you authority status. Items eight through 12 on the list above are things that you can do without anyone else's permission to build your authority. All you need is initiative.

WHAT CAN YOU START DOING NOW
TO BUILD MORE AUTHORITY?

SUCCESS PRINCIPLE #9: BE REMARKABLE

> "I've learned that people will forget what you said, people will forget what you did, but people will never forget how you made them feel."
>
> **— MAYA ANGELOU**

There's a popular book called *Purple Cow* by Seth Godin. The thesis is that we are living in a New Economy and the old way of doing business doesn't cut it anymore. In other words, offering a good product or doing a good job isn't good enough – you have to be remarkable. For professionals, this can be interpreted as delivering a remarkable client or patient experience.

First, let's touch on why delivering a remarkable experience is a success principle. The fact that something is remarkable means that people will remark on or talk about it. What you say or do may give the impression of being innovative, thoughtful, exciting – whatever it is creates buzz. Providing remarkable experiences in turn generates referral and repeat business.

Furthermore, it's difficult to place a value on remarkable experiences. I will illustrate this point with an example.

Imagine that your 5-year old son had a bad experience at a dental clinic. Now he's afraid to go back to the dentist. Your friend recommended a different clinic where she takes her kids and you pray it's better than the last. The best-case scenario is that your son gets over his fear. The worst-case scenario is that the new clinic reinforces his fear, causing him to throw tantrums and avoid the dentist forevermore.

Your son is visibly nervous as you drive him to his check-up, but you are both put at ease when you walk into the clinic. The receptionist greets you warmly and offers comfortable seating near a glowing fireplace. Your son starts playing on the rocking chair in the children's play space. Instead of the usual robotic phone answering, you hear staff responding to inquiries with genuine empathy as you wait for the appointment.

When the hygienist appears, she knows you and your son by name. She greets your son in a friendly manner and chats to him like a pro, keeping him engaged and at ease. She ushers you both to the dentist's office where she shows him the tools and explains why they use them. Once he sees there's no reason to be scared, she walks him through his cleaning and it's over before he knows it. The equally friendly dentist pops in, establishes rapport, has a quick look in your son's mouth, and delivers a loot bag including bubbles, stickers, a bouncy toy, and tooth brush. Feeling relieved and so happy to see your son unphased, you schedule his next appointment before leaving the clinic.

How much is your son's positive experience worth to you? While it may be difficult to place a monetary value on this experience, it's fair to say that it's worth a lot, especially in comparison to the alternative. That's why positive experiences enable professional practices to attract avatar clients and patients and charge higher than normal fees.

While it may look easy, a seamless client or patient experience is a result of vigilantly implemented and dutifully monitored systems. It does not happen naturally.

A business-owner friend once told me about an accountant who opened his office in her neighbourhood. He went up and down the street handing out fresh pies to all his neighbours. Now that's a remarkable introduction.

The husband and wife owners of Breyer Law Offices also do a superb job of delivering remarkable client experiences. First, you should know that Mark and Alexis are out-going and upbeat, so the experiences they deliver align with their personalities. One of the things you'll notice when walking into their beautiful offices is their numerous awards framed and mounted on the walls. There are also several magazines with cover features of the husband and wife team. It's impossible to miss the fully stocked all-you-can-eat ice cream bar in reception.

If that's not enough to impress, the Breyers host quarterly events for their VIP clients, which by the way, is almost every client. One time they rented a movie theatre and gave away free movie tickets and popcorn. They've also hosted Casino Nights. Recently, they introduced an annual Spring Carnival where they set up bouncy castles, rides, and games in their office parking lot, complete with Mark in the dunk tank (I'm not kidding). It's fun for the whole family.

The Breyers are experts at creating remarkable client experiences and equally expert at leveraging these experiences to generate referral and repeat business. Not only are people talking about their fun-filled experiences for days (or years), they're writing Google reviews and testimonials at the events. Visit their Facebook Page @HusbandAndWifeLawTeam to discover more of the incredible stuff they do.

I'm not saying you have to install an ice cream bar in your reception or host a carnival every spring in order to deliver remarkable experiences. Certainly not.

I'm challenging you to think carefully about the experiences you want to create and find ways to make clients and patients feel special. While it may seem like a lot of work now, soon it will be routine and you will be rewarded with more and better business.

WHAT KIND OF EXPERIENCE DO YOU WANT YOUR CLIENTS OR PATIENTS TO HAVE WITH YOU? HOW CAN YOU MAKE THEIR EXPERIENCE REMARKABLE?

SUCCESS PRINCIPLE #10: NURTURE YOUR RELATIONSHIPS

> "A monthly print newsletter is the single easiest and most effective way to increase retention rates, increase referrals, and instantly build long-lasting relationships with your clients." **– SHAUN BUCK**

I've mentioned before that I used to be the in-house marketing director for a small law firm in St. John's, Newfoundland and Labrador. After increasing our target intake by 94% in three years, my employer sold his practice and licensed the firm name. That gave me the opportunity to help professionals across North America with their marketing operations so they, too, can bring their dreams to life. That's when I founded Proven Marketing for Professionals and I've been Canada's *only* education-based marketing consultant exclusively for professionals ever since.

The funny thing is, hindsight is 20/20. Even though I helped to build a highly successful law firm, so successful that my employer sold the practice, I see what we should have done to get better results even sooner.

I say with complete confidence that our first and most focused marketing effort should have been a monthly newsletter. I know from experience that newsletter marketing should be your most fundamental marketing system, too. Here are the top five reasons why:

1. **You get more referrals and quality business**. Business owners agree that referrals are the best type of business. A great newsletter keeps you top of mind and turns people into raving fans. You get more inquiries and accept only the most profitable and gratifying clients and patients.

2. **You get more repeat business**. The main reason why satisfied clients and patients don't return is because they've forgotten about you. Doing an interesting newsletter keeps you in front of people so that they remember and come back to you.

3. **You have fewer management hassles and break-ups**. A newsletter puts you in regular contact with clients and patients – even when you have no news specifically for them. Not only does this foster stronger client or patient loyalty, you have fewer management hassles and break-ups.

4. **It helps build your brand**. Your brand is the complex network of emotions that you represent in the minds of others. A newsletter helps you develop that network with consistent communication, always leaving readers with a great impression.

5. **NOT doing a newsletter is money lost**. Most business owners fail to leverage their most valuable asset – the relationships they've already created. Not maintaining your relationships is to ignore the highest return on investment that you can make in your business's future.

There are a few important things to understand here. First, I'm not talking about any old newsletter. The truth is, most newsletters are boring and that's the biggest mistake you can make. *I'm talking about a fun-to-read newsletter.* Newsletters that are fun-to-read share personality, jokes, stories, quotes, recipes, and other cool stuff. No more than 20% of content is about your products or services.

Second, your newsletter shouldn't be delivered to just anyone. *It should go to people who already know, like, and trust you.* That means former and current clients or patients, strategic partners, family, and friends. Because they already know, like, and trust you, these people are likely to refer and return to you when they need your help.

A third point to understand relates to media. Most people think about email when it comes to newsletter marketing, but the truth is, *when done properly, a printed and mailed newsletter generates a much higher return on investment.* Open rates and attention spans on email are low. Printed and mailed newsletters show up in less crowded mailboxes and stick around homes and offices.

Last but not least, a word on frequency. You can't expect much from a quarterly newsletter or something you send sporadically. *It must be consistent – monthly is the gold standard.* Only when you stay top-of-mind will people remember, refer, and return to you.

A lot of people resist doing fun-to-read newsletters. Some people say they're too much work. Some people say they're too expensive. Some people say it's a silly idea. I say, more market share for the rest of us.

When I was an in-house marketing director, we didn't quite believe it would work, either. At first, we did it sporadically and were unconvinced. Finally, we decided to give it our best shot and test it once and for all. We figured that if the newsletter wasn't showing concrete results after one year, we'd scrap it. We added unique tracking phone numbers to all of our media, including the newsletter.

Once we were producing a monthly printed and mailed newsletter, our referral and repeat business increased – not just a little – a lot. It helped that we added as many people to our mailing list as possible. Soon we realized that the newsletter was our **top call source** every single month. In other words, it became our most valuable marketing asset. If you don't believe me, here are just a few original comments we received from readers…

"I thoroughly enjoy the newsletters and look forward to receiving them. I've had numerous people inquire of me the names of good personal injury lawyers and I have no hesitation in referring [your law firm] to them. Thank you. You're The Best."

Georgina

"As a registered massage therapist I see many people injured in MVA's and find your newsletters very informative and I share the content along with my own experience as a therapist when it comes to injuries and the rights of the victim. Thank you for sending me those newsletters! I also enjoy the other articles you include, the recipes, and of course the opportunity of getting

to know your staff. It makes things so much more personal and it seems like a fantastic place to work!... I'm not sure that you have received any of my clients but I do encourage them!"

Debbie

"Just a little note saying how I love the newsletters. I really enjoy reading them and how you make every effort to apply yourself to help people. I have learned a lot from just reading them. Thank you so much. Thumbs up to you all. Doing a great job!!!!"

Kimberly

"Just wanted to let you know, even though I have not had to avail of your services I enjoy reading the newsletters I get in the mail and will call on you if ever I need help :) Your name is certainly well known!! Thanks."

Jackie

"Just a little note to say thank you for the newsletter that I receive. Lots of info that I am learning. I especially enjoy the recipes – the cookie recipe in the last issue was terrific. Look forward to the next copy. Keep up the good work in letting public know. P.S. give Fox a big hug and kiss for me. He looks so, so sweet, and adorable. Merry Christmas and Happy New Year to you and your staff."

Alice

"We receive your newsletter and enjoy reading it very much. It's good to be informed about the service you provide people. If ever in need of a lawyer we would know who to call."

Charles

"Thanks so much for sending me your newsletters. Not only do they have invaluable information but have great recipes as well. I have tried the cheese cake & blueberry oatmeal cookie recipes. They are to die for! Pls. keep the newsletters coming."

Cathy

"I love receiving the newsletter. I have been getting them for a few years now and read every word…"

Wanda

"I enjoy reading your forum whenever I receive them, they are so informative, and it is so consoling to realize that there is a competent and willing source to turn to for information and assistance."

Terry

"I LOVED it. Catherine, the newsletter was great! Loved the part about the cats too!"

Alexis

I know hundreds of small business owners across North America who send a monthly printed and mailed newsletter. Furthermore, they report it to be their most valuable marketing asset and the last effort they'd give up if they had to slash their marketing budget. A printed and mailed newsletter was the first form of marketing I did when I started my company in 2016 and I still do it today, for good reason.

If a consistent, fun-to-read, printed and mailed newsletter is not for you, find other ways to nurture your relationships.

SUCCESS PRINCIPLE #11: WORK SMART

> "I know of no more encouraging fact than the unquestionable ability of man to elevate his life by conscious endeavor." **– HENRY DAVID THOREAU**

I'll start this chapter with a story about a professional development event I attended once. It was a conference, so there were various speakers discussing a multitude of topics. A couple of take-home messages stood out, and I was sorely disappointed with them.

One of the messages was, "If you want to get ahead, you just have to put your head down and work harder." Surely a big group of smart professionals can come up with better advice than that!

Working harder and longer hours *might* help you make more money. It will *not* help you get home in time for dinner, make it to your kid's soccer games, have more time with an aging parent, or give you longer weekends at the cottage. No, sir.

The dysfunctional mindset of "just work harder" is one of the main reasons why many professionals are unhappy and suffering from health problems. It creates burn-out, the consequences of which include loss of productivity, errors in judgement, business-killing claims, regulatory troubles, and high turn-over rates.

Because you're reading this book, I'm going to assume that working harder and longer hours will not help you achieve your version of success.

You want to accomplish more in less time. To do that you have to work smarter. That's the advice that should have been shared at the conference I attended.

Working smart starts with doing what *only you* can do. Whether you own a practice that provides professional services or you're a young associate, you must commit to doing only the highest-value work for your time. Delegate and outsource everything else.

An essential part of this process is building a super-star team, so that everything you delegate or outsource is completed to your standard. That means hiring slow, firing fast, and training all the time.

It involves creating and refining systems. Do you have scripts for intake staff? Do you a have a follow-up process for warm leads? Do you have a step-by-step onboarding system for new clients or patients? Do you have a systematic way of managing client or patient expectations? Do you have templates for communications? Are your services scalable? These are just a few ways to create efficiencies.

Working smart also involves using technology to optimize performance. Technology resources are available to make your life easier. You should use them to grow your productivity, earnings, and free time exponentially.

Keep in mind, this isn't easy. Most business owners say that the hardest part about growth is managing people. However, when you learn to do it well, you discover first-hand that leadership, management, and systems are the keys to a prosperous and happy business life.

Lawyer Ben Glass is one of a few work smart experts in my life. Lawyers can learn more about working smart and practice-building at **CatherineLovesGLM.com**.

AT YOUR OFFICE, WHAT ARE THE TASKS
THAT *ONLY YOU* CAN DO? WHAT DO YOU
DO THAT YOU SHOULDN'T? WHO SHOULD
BE DOING THIS LOWER VALUE WORK?

SUCCESS PRINCIPLE
#12: TAKE ACTION

> "Sometimes when I consider what tremendous consequences come from little things... I am tempted to think... there are no little things." **– BRUCE BARTON**

There's a great book called *The Slight Edge*. Author Jeff Olson explains that success is not a matter of luck, timing, or fate. Neither is it a matter of intelligence, skill, or talent. The reason why some people succeed while others don't is a difference in philosophy, or how they think.

> *A positive philosophy turns into a positive attitude, which turns into positive actions, which turns into positive results, which turns into a positive lifestyle.*

> *A negative philosophy turns into a negative attitude, which turns into negative actions, which turns into negative results, which turns into a negative lifestyle.*

That's why this book focuses on mindset. However, there's another essential component to success that I wish to highlight. Olson also explains that where you end up is the result of **consistent action compounded over time**.

Let's think about that for a minute. Whether you succeed is the result of your daily *habits* and the momentum they create over years of *doing* (or not doing). Your simple everyday *actions* either drive you forward or backward with compounding power. There's no such thing as standing still.

This guide gives you the mindset tools and some practical ideas to help you design your life your way. You're half way there. Now you have to create momentum by putting things in motion. You have to take the ideas in this guide and *act* on them to bring your dreams to life.

By the way, everyone falls off the wagon sometimes. There are any number of legitimate reasons why. Just hop back on.

Like Olson says, it's never too late to start. It's always too late to wait.

Just imagine where the power of compounding results could land you in 2 years, 5 years, or 10 years if you start turning these ideas into action today.

One more thing – I have a special offer to make this easier...

Proven Marketing for Professionals sends a printed and mailed newsletter to a select group of professionals who are dedicated to building a better practice.

In it, I share valuable insights to help professionals succeed, great tips, useful resources, plus other "fun stuff" like quotes and recipes. (If you read the chapter on nurturing your relationships, you'll see I practice what I preach).

Visit **www.BringDreamsToLifeNewsletter.com** and enter your mailing address to get a complimentary subscription, as my gift to you. It will help you on your journey.

> "When you are eighty years old, and in a quiet moment of reflection narrating for only yourself the most personal version of your life story, the telling that will be most compact and meaningful will be the series of choices you have made. In the end, we are our choices." **– JEFF BEZOS**

BONUS CHAPTER: HOW WE DID IT

At the beginning of this guide I told you about how I worked at my father's law firm, Ches Crosbie Barristers, as Marketing Director. I also told you that during these three years our target intake skyrocketed by 94%. The marketing systems that I implemented allowed my father to focus on practicing law, without doubting that there would be a reliable stream of cash flow cases being opened on a monthly basis. The firm became a saleable asset because of its marketing systems that attracted regular business, and he sold the practice in 2016. So, how did we do it?

In the last chapter I explained that taking consistent action towards your goals creates exponential growth over time. Well, at Ches Crosbie Barristers we took steady massive action. In other words, we cranked up the volume.

My father was able to nearly double his target intake and sell the practice because he had a marketing director who "gets it". He put in the foundational mindset work outlined in this book, and because I was on the same page, we were able to work in tandem to reach his goals. Furthermore, I was able to accomplish multiple times what he was able to accomplish without marketing support (he had cases to win, after all).

If you're interested in multiplying your efforts with the help of a marketing gal who "gets it", get in touch to schedule a complimentary Prospective Client Interview. This 30-minute appointment is an opportunity to see whether and how I can help you. Email **Hello@CatherineCrosbie.com** or call 902–453–1903 to schedule your interview today.

SUGGESTED READING

If you're serious about building a better practice, you need to study marketing, business, and success. Below is a list of some of my favourite books. Start reading!

Renegade Lawyer Marketing, *Ben Glass*

Outrageous Advertising, *Bill Glazer*

Deep Work, *Cal Newport*

Never Split the Difference, *Chris Voss*

The Ultimate Marketing Plan, *Dan Kennedy*

No B.S. Direct Marketing, *Dan Kennedy*

No B.S. Wealth Attraction In The New Economy, *Dan Kennedy*

No B.S. Sales Success In The New Economy, *Dan Kennedy*

No B.S. Guide To Direct Response Social Media Marketing, *Dan Kennedy and Kim Walsh-Phillips*

A New Earth, *Eckhart Tolle*

Good to Great, *Jim Collins*

The Slight Edge, *Jeff Olson*

The 7 Habits of Highly Effective People, *Stephen Covey*

The Phone Book, *Mary Jane Copps*

Profit First, *Mike Michalowicz*

Think and Grow Rich, *Napoleon Hill*

StorySelling, *Nick Nanton and JW Dicks*

Celebrity Branding You, *Nick Nanton, Jack Dicks, and Lindsay Dicks*

Fascinate, *Sally Hogshead*

Purple Cow, *Seth Godin*

Everybody Lies, *Seth Stephens-Davidowitz*

www.ingramcontent.com/pod-product-compliance
Lightning Source LLC
Chambersburg PA
CBHW021957190326
41519CB00009B/1304